Our National Parks

By
Teri Crawford Jones

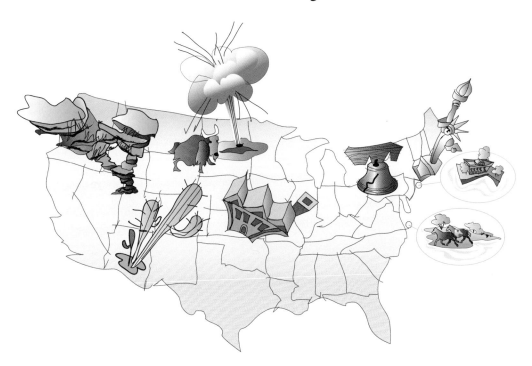

MODERN CURRICULUM PRESS
Pearson Learning Group

The following people have contributed to the development of this product:

Art and Design: Stephen Barth, Susan Brorein, Salita Mehta, Elizabeth Nemeth, Alison O'Brien

Editorial: Leslie Feierstone Barna, Nicole Iorio, Jennie Rakos, Jennifer Serra

Inventory: Levon Carter

Marketing: Alison Bruno

Production: Roxanne Knoll

ISBN-13: 978-1-4284-0819-7
ISBN-10: 1-4284-0819-3

Printed in the United States of America
1 2 3 4 5 6 7 8 9 10   11 10 09 08 07

Pearson Learning Group

1-800-321-3106
www.pearsonlearning.com

Contents

America's Parks

People go to parks in all of America's states. They can visit parks in the city and in the country. Some parks are by the sea, and others are in the **desert**.

Almost every state has **national** parks. People pay to go to some parks. Other parks are free.

America has 390 national parks. One state has 30 parks. Two states have just four.

◀ Big rocks are just one thing to see at national parks.

Country Parks

Some parks are home to special kinds of plants and animals. If these places were not made into parks, then many plants and animals would not have a home. They might die.

A Desert Park

One national park in Arizona is in the hot desert. In this park a tall **cactus** lives. These big plants can be 50 feet tall and live 150 years. Many kinds of desert animals live in just one cactus. If we did not have this national park in Arizona, this kind of cactus might not live. Then the desert animals who need the cactus might not have food or a home.

This national park
saves land for this
special kind of cactus.

People can see geysers
at Yellowstone.

A One-of-a-Kind Park

Yellowstone is a park people like to visit.
Yellowstone has many **geysers**. Geysers are
holes in the Earth out of which comes a
big rush of hot water high up into the air.
People like to see the geysers. Yellowstone
has miles and miles of trees. Many large
animals live in Yellowstone.

An Island Park

Part of an **island** in Maryland is a special national park. The island has sand and tall grass. People once lived on the island. In the past horses came with people to this Maryland island. Some horses got away and learned to live without people. Now there are about 300 horses that live on the island.

There are many things to see and do at country parks. People can camp, fish, and hike. At national parks in Arizona, Maryland, and other states, people can see many different kinds of animals and plants.

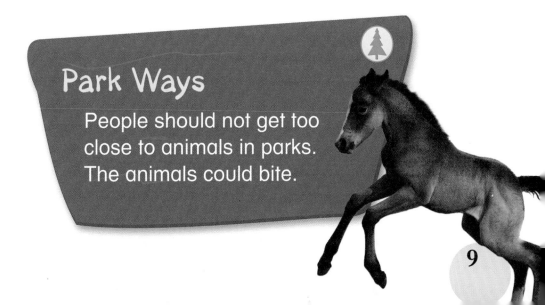

Park Ways

People should not get too close to animals in parks. The animals could bite.

9

City Parks

People often visit the big national parks in the country. There are also parks to visit in cities. People can learn about America's **history** at many of these city parks.

Philadelphia, Pennsylvania, is an important city in our history. A national park in Philadelphia is as big as 20 city blocks. This Pennsylvania park has places that show how our nation began.

One place in Philadelphia, Pennsylvania, is home to a very old bell. The bell was once called the State House bell. When people visit this national park, they think about how our country became free.

People can visit a very old bell at a national park in Philadelphia.

Parks With History

One school in Topeka, Kansas, is important in our history. Before 1954 black children and white children in some places went to different schools. Some people in Topeka, Kansas, wanted all children to go to school together. They went to **court**. In 1954 the high court of our nation said that black children and white children could be in one school.

This school in Topeka, Kansas, with so much history, closed in 1975. In 1992 the school became a national park. People can visit the school to learn its important story. When people visit, they think about how the courts can change our country.

Some people in Kansas went to court so black children and white children could go to school together.

13

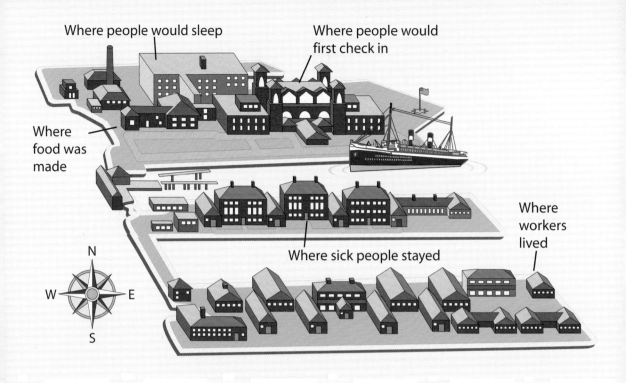

Where people would sleep

Where people would first check in

Where food was made

Where workers lived

Where sick people stayed

N
W   E
S

▲ This is how Ellis Island worked when it was a check in for new Americans.

Near New York City is Ellis Island. Ellis Island is a national park that was important to many people who came to America between 1892 and 1954. These people came by ship from many parts of the world. They left their homes in other countries. They came to America so they could be free. They wanted to have a new life.

The people had to go to Ellis Island near New York City first to find out if they could stay in America. Some had to stay on the island because they were sick. When they were well, they could go on to New York City and other parts of America. Many children today hear about how their families came to America through Ellis Island.

National parks like Ellis Island help us learn about the people that made our country great. People can learn a lot about important times and what our country was like in the past. These parks keep our history for people to see in years to come.

Park Ways

After Ellis Island was closed, it was soon very run down. It was an important place, so people worked hard to fix it.

Glossary

cactus a kind of plant that grows in dry places and has spikes

court a place where people are made to follow the rules of a state or the nation

desert a dry, hot place with rock and sand and few plants

geysers springs that send jets of hot water and steam into the air

history what people did in the past

island land that has water on all sides

national having to do with a country